FUN FINDING OUT

ME AND MY WORLD

Rosie McCormick   Anthony Lewis

KING*f*ISHER

To Suzanne – RMC

To Nana – AL

KINGFISHER
Kingfisher Publications Plc
New Penderel House, 283–288 High Holborn, London WC1V 7HZ

First published by Kingfisher Publications Plc 1998
This edition published 2000
10 9 8 7 6 5 4 3 2 1
1(TR)/1099/TWP/FR/130ARM

A CIP catalogue
record for this book is available
from the British Library.

ISBN 0 7534 0454 0

The rights of Rosie McCormick to be
identified as author of this book and
Anthony Lewis to be identified as
illustrator of this book have been
asserted by them in accordance with
the Copyright, Designs and Patents
Act, 1988.

Series editor: Sue Nicholson
Series designer: Kathryn Caulfield

Printed in Singapore

Answers

Who came first?
Great-grandfather;
Grandfather; Dad; Baby

Who does which job?
Vet – heals animals
Hairdresser – cuts hair
Chef – cooks food

Where do these foods come from?
Ketchup – tomatoes
Omelette – Eggs
Chips – Potatoes

Where are these children going?
1 Football pitch
2 Tennis court
3 Swimming pool

The right clothes
1 Raincoat, hat and
  wellington boots
2 Sunhat, sunglasses, sandals,
  T-shirt and shorts
3 Warm hat, scarf and
  gloves; warm coat and
  trousers

Contents

Me and my family

Most children live with their families. Families take care of each other, love each other and have fun together. Being with people who love and respect you is very important.

My grandfather – he's my mum's dad.

My grandmother – she's my mum's mum.

My grandmother – she's my dad's mum.

My dad

My mum

My sister

My baby brother

ME

My great-grandfather – he's my grandmother's dad.

Pets are important members of a family, too!

My uncle – he's my mum's brother.

My cousins – they're my aunt and uncle's children.

Some children's parents are divorced. When this happens, children may live with their mum…

…or with their dad. But they usually get to spend a lot of time with both parents.

Some children are adopted by parents who didn't give birth to them, but who love them very, very much.

My aunt – she's my dad's sister.

My grandfather – he's my dad's dad.

My other cousin

Who came first?

To work out who came first, look for the oldest person.

Grandfather

Baby

Great-grandfather

Dad

Where I live

People live in all kinds of places. Some live in big, busy cities with enormous buildings that seem to touch the sky. Others live in towns, small villages or in the countryside. Where do you live?

Some people live and work on farms in the countryside.

A town is smaller than a city. It has fewer buildings, and fewer people live there.

A village is smaller than a town. Some villages are so small that many of the people who live there know each other.

A city is a large, important centre. Cars, buses and trains bring people into the city and help them get around quickly. Some cities have airports, too.

Many people move to cities from towns or the countryside. Cities usually have more jobs, schools and places to live.

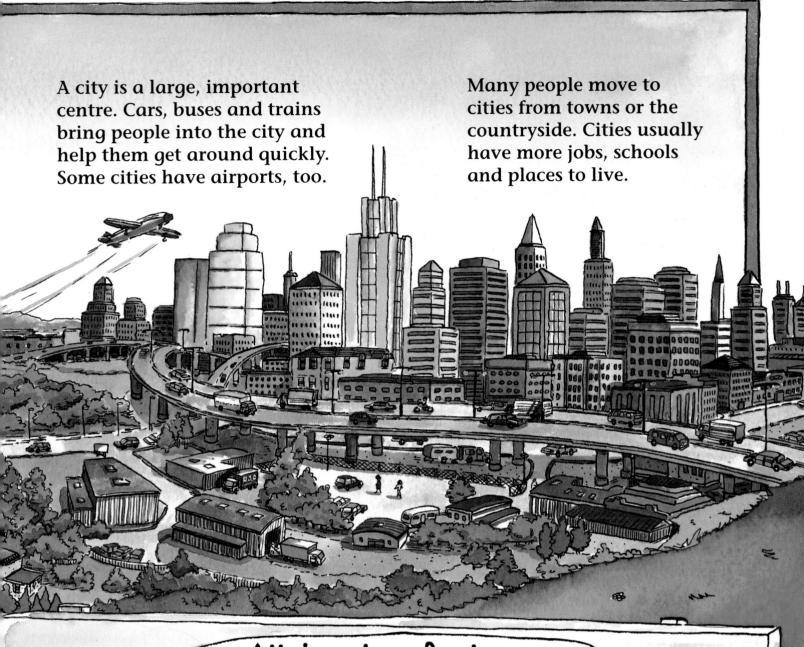

All kinds of places

People live in different places and in different ways all over the world.

Some people live in cold, snowy places.

Some people live in hot, sunny places.

Some people live by the sea.

My home

Homes come in many different shapes and sizes. A home can be a house, a flat or a caravan. But no matter where you live, home is the place you share with your family.

In most homes, there are rules about tidying-up and being nice to each other. Rules make it easier to live together.

Living together can sometimes be difficult. But it's all part of belonging to a family.

Attic

Bathroom

Bedroom

Living room

Kitchen

All kinds of homes

Some people live in a flat in a large building called a block of flats.

Some people live in wooden houses called cabins.

Some people live in a caravan in a caravan park.

My bedroom

If you are lucky, you may have your very own bedroom where you can keep your favourite things.

Some houses have a garage for parking the car and storing tools.

Building a house

Every year, thousands of new homes are built for people to live in. Building a new house is hard work. There are lots of different jobs to do and each job is done by a skilled worker.

First, the foundations, which help to support the building, are dug into the ground. Next, gas and water pipes are put down.

Builders at work

The bricklayer builds the walls with brick. The bricks are held together with cement.

The carpenter uses wood for the floor and to make frames for the doors and windows.

The roofer uses tiles to make the roof. Often, the tiles are made out of slate.

Have you and your family ever moved house? Moving to a new house is exciting, but it's also hard work.

When you move, you have to pack up all of your things. They are often carried to your new house by van.

The architect and the site foreman check the building plans to make sure that the work is being done properly.

The plumber connects the house's water and gas pipes with main pipes outside.

The electrician puts in wires to carry electricity to the lights and the wall sockets.

The plasterer coats the walls with plaster. The painter paints them when they are dry.

Jobs people do

In every city, town and village, there are people doing all kinds of jobs. Some people's jobs are to look after us. Doctors and nurses care for us when we are sick. The police and firefighters keep us safe.

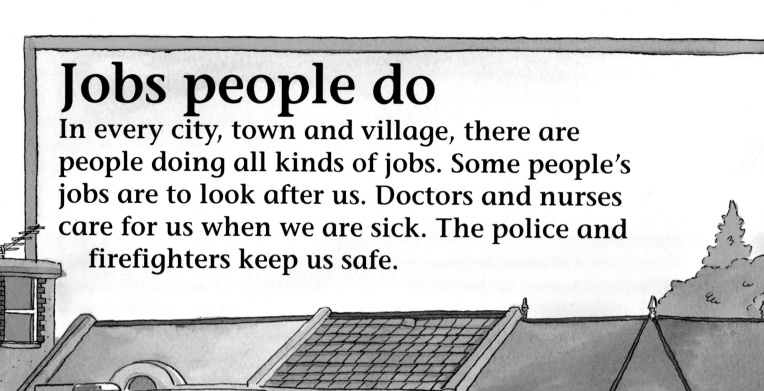

Bus drivers drive buses which carry people from place to place.

Doctors, nurses and ambulance staff look after us if we are sick or have an accident.

The police catch people who break the law. They make sure our streets and homes are safe.

Mechanics check car engines and repair them if they break down.

Shopkeepers and shop assistants help us to find what we want when we go shopping. They also take our money and give us our change at a till.

Firefighters put out dangerous fires and rescue people (and sometimes pets) in trouble.

Who does which job?

Vet

Hairdresser

Chef

Cuts hair

Cooks food

Heals animals

Going shopping

Everything you eat, wear and use is bought in a shop. There are lots of small shops selling food, clothes or toys. And there are giant stores that sell almost everything!

Lots of people work in a giant store or a supermarket doing different jobs.

Some people work on the tills at the check-out. They add up the cost of the shopping.

Can you find these things?

Fruit

Newspapers

Fish

Some people make sure that the shelves are always full.

Some people work behind special counters selling bread and cakes, fish, meat or cheese.

Things I eat

What do you like to eat? Food gives you energy, keeps you healthy and helps you to grow big and strong. But do you know where the food you eat comes from?

Most of the food you eat is grown in the countryside. Farmers grow crops and vegetables and raise animals for meat.

Most fruits, such as pears and apples, grow on trees. They are picked when they are ready to eat.

Vegetables include beans, carrots, potatoes and peas. Most are cooked to make them softer to eat.

Cereal crops include wheat, barley and corn. From wheat, we make bread, cereal and pasta.

Where do these foods come from?

Ketchup

Omelette

Chips

Potatoes

Eggs

Tomatoes

Farm animals, such as chickens, give us meat. Chickens also provide us with eggs.

Dairy cows give us milk. From milk, we can make butter, cheese, yoghurt and ice cream.

Most cheese is made from cow's milk. But it can also be made from goat's and sheep's milk.

Going to school

Do you go to school? Some children start school when they are about three years old. Others begin when they are five or six. At school, you learn to read, write, count and paint – and you make lots of friends!

Learning how to count is very important. It's also lots of fun. First you learn how to count to 10, then to 20, and soon you can count up to 100 and more! How high can you count?

At school, you learn how to paint with a brush, and how to mix paints to make different colours.

Exercise helps to keep you fit and healthy. You may learn how to climb bars or even a rope!

The alphabet is the first thing you learn when you are learning how to read.

When you know all of the letters, you can put them together to make words.

19

Things I like to do

Most people have a favourite game
they like to play or a special hobby.
Some people enjoy reading, painting
or making models. Others like sports,
such as football or horse-riding.
What do you like to do?

Kite-
flying

Leap-frog

Baseball

Football

Where are these children going?

1

2

3

Football pitch

Swimming pool

Tennis court

20

Horse-riding

Roller-skating

Tennis

Drawing

Dancing

Computer games

Reading

My pets

Looking after a pet can be great fun, and some pets become special friends. But remember, all pets need special care and attention – and lots of love.

Snakes

Tarantulas

Stick insects

Mice

Hamsters

Guinea pigs

Puppies are full of energy. They need to be trained to live indoors.

Rabbits can live outside in a roomy hutch with space for them to hop and run.

Taking care of pets

Keeping a pet can take up a lot of your time.

Cats need fresh food and water – and someone to play with.

Dogs need healthy food and lots of exercise. They need to be groomed, too.

Hamsters need to have clean cages and fresh straw for bedding.

Cats and kittens make good pets. But like dogs and puppies, they need lots of loving care.

Fish need feeding every day and their tanks must be kept clean.

The weather

What's the weather like today? In many places, the weather is always changing. From sunshine and rainbows, to rain and snow, the weather affects our lives and how we feel. Sunshine can make us feel happy. In frosty weather, we may shiver and shake with cold.

The weather affects what we wear. Clothes can keep us cool when it is hot and warm when it is cold.

The right clothes

What would you wear if it was...

1 Cool and rainy?

2 Hot and sunny?

3 Cold and snowy?

Rumble

It's fun to play in the snow, but we need to dress warmly.

In hot weather, we need to keep cool and use lots of suncream.

When heavy clouds bring thunderstorms, it's best to stay indoors!

On wet, windy days, we may need to wear raincoats, and waterproof boots to keep our feet dry.

Growing things

Plants are an important part of our world. They grow in gardens, parks and fields. They make our world green and colourful. Some plants also provide us with food.

Plants make their own food from water, a gas in the air called carbon dioxide, and sunlight.

Sunflowers

Poppies

Daisies

Watch a seed grow

See how a plant's leaves grow towards the light.

Bean

Fill a glass jar with water, line it with blotting paper, and place a broad bean seed between the paper and the jar.

Soon, tiny white roots will start to grow down towards the ground, and a small green shoot will push up towards the light.

Apple tree

Just like all living things, plants need water and food to give them energy to grow.

Runner beans

Tomatoes

Mint

Parsley

Bay

A large tree has much bigger, longer roots than a small flower.

Most plants have roots to take in water. Some, like potatoes, store food in stems called tubers.

Aster

Potatoes

Roots

Tubers

Celebrations

An important part of life is celebrating the nice things that happen. That's why there are birthdays to remember the day that we were born. Celebrations remind us that there are lots of things to be happy about.

On your birthday, you may have a party to celebrate with your family and friends.

They give you cards and presents...

... and you all dress in your best party clothes.

It's time to celebrate!

Every country celebrates its own special holidays.

In the United States, families share a special feast to celebrate Thanksgiving Day.

In Japan, some families fly colourful streamers from their homes to celebrate Children's Day.

In West Africa, the Homowo Festival celebrates the birth of twins.

A birthday cake, with flickering candles, tells everyone how old you are.

My world at night

While you are tucked up in bed, safe and warm, the world outside your window is as busy as ever. Some people go to work just as you are closing your eyes to go to sleep.

Train drivers drive the trains that carry our letters and parcels through the night.

Police and fire stations stay open all night long in case there are any emergencies.

While you're asleep...

Bakers bake bread and cakes so that they will be fresh for people to buy the next day.

Postal workers sort out the post so that our letters and parcels will arrive on time.

Printers print newspapers so that we can read the most up-to-date news in the morning.

Hospitals must stay open all the time. Doctors and nurses take turns to work through the night.

Many petrol stations stay open, too, so that people travelling late at night can buy petrol.

Index